Cultural Traditions in
Israel

Molly
Aloian

Crabtree Publishing Company

Crabtree Publishing Company

www.crabtreebooks.com

Author: Molly Aloian
Publishing plan research and development:
 Reagan Miller
Editors: Kelly Spence, Adrianna Morganelli
Proofreaders: Marcia Abramson, Wendy Scavuzzo
Design: Tibor Choleva
Photo research: Melissa McClellan
Production coordinator and prepress technician:
 Tammy McGarr
Print coordinator: Margaret Amy Salter

Produced and Designed by BlueAppleWorks Inc.

Cover: Torah Scroll (middle left); menorah (bottom right); Olive tree (background left); Bar Mitzvah ritual (center); Masada in the desert of Israel (background); Rosh Ha Shana. Apples and Honey (bottom left)

Title page: Unidentified Israel Scouts at Tel Aviv beach

Photographs:
Dreamstime: © Sergey02: title page; © Aleksandar Todorovic: page 4; © Lucidwaters: page 8; © Tomert: page 9 (bottom); © Noam Armonn: pages 10 (bottom), 31 (top); © Blueenayim: page 11 (bottom); © Gorshkov13: page 15; © Dmitrydesigner: page 23 (bottom)
Keystone Press: © Jane V Windsor/St. Petersburg Times/ZUMA Press: page 22
Shutterstock: Cover (all): © umbertoleporini (bottom right); © Deyan Georgiev (background left); © Sean Pavone (background); © Boris-B (bottom left); © dnaveh: title page (bottom), page 7; © ChameleonsEye: cover (center), pages 5, 8 (background), 12 (inset), 13, 14, 18 (bottom), 20 (inset), 23 (top), 26 (bottom & inset), 27, 29 (top); © littleny: page 6; © Protasov AN: pages 6-7 (background), 26-27 (background); © Vitaliy Berkovych page 9; © Maglara: page 11; © Corky Buczyk: page 12; © Eldad Carin: page 12 (top); © Boris Diakovsky: page 16 (bottom left); © FotoYakov: pages 16-17 (background); © dnaveh pages 16-17 (bottom); © Vadim Petrakov: page 18 (background); © ZouZou: page 19; © Terence Mendoza: page 20; © Flik47: page 21 (background); © mikhail: cover (middle left), page 21 (inset); © Paolo Bona: page 24; © Maksim Dubinsky: page 24 (bottom); © kavram: page 25 (background), 27 (bottom); © Arkady Mazor: page 25 (bottom); © Aleksandar Todorovic: page 28; © silver-john: page 29; © arka38: page 30; © Lisa F. Young: page 31
Wikimedia Commons: Gilabrand: page 7 (inset)

Library and Archives Canada Cataloguing in Publication

Aloian, Molly, author
 Cultural traditions in Israel / Molly Aloian.

(Cultural traditions in my world)
Includes index.
Issued in print and electronic formats.
ISBN 978-0-7787-0303-7 (bound).--ISBN 978-0-7787-0315-0 (pbk.).--
ISBN 978-1-4271-7487-1 (html).--ISBN 978-1-4271-7493-2 (pdf)

 1. Holidays--Israel--Juvenile literature. 2. Fasts and feasts--
Judaism--Juvenile literature. 3. Israel--Social life and customs--
Juvenile literature. I. Title. II. Series: Cultural traditions in my
world

GT4874.5.I7A56 2014   j394.2695694   C2014-900909-7
                                         C2014-900910-0

Library of Congress Cataloging-in-Publication Data

Aloian, Molly.
 Cultural traditions in Israel / Molly Aloian.
  pages cm. -- (Cultural traditions in my world)
 Includes index.
 ISBN 978-0-7787-0303-7 (reinforced library binding : alk. paper) -- ISBN 978-0-7787-0315-0 (pbk. : alk. paper) -- ISBN 978-1-4271-7493-2 (electronic pdf : alk. paper) -- ISBN 978-1-4271-7487-1 (electronic html : alk. paper)
 1. Holidays--Israel--Juvenile literature. 2. Festivals--Israel--Juvenile literature. 3. Israel--Social life and customs--Juvenile literature. I. Title.

 GT4886.I7A46 2014
 394.2695694--dc23

                         2014005117

Crabtree Publishing Company

www.crabtreebooks.com   1-800-387-7650

Printed in the USA/052014/SN20140313

Published in Canada
Crabtree Publishing
616 Welland Ave.
St. Catharines, ON
L2M 5V6

Published in the United States
Crabtree Publishing
PMB 59051
350 Fifth Avenue, 59th Floor
New York, New York 10118

Published in the United Kingdom
Crabtree Publishing
Maritime House
Basin Road North, Hove
BN41 1WR

Published in Australia
Crabtree Publishing
3 Charles Street
Coburg North
VIC 3058

Contents

Welcome to Israel

Israel is a small country in the Middle East with a long history and unique culture. It is about the same size as New Jersey. Over seven million people live in Israel. Almost three quarters of the population is Jewish, but there are also Muslims and Christians living there. The two official languages in Israel are Hebrew and Arabic.

Israel's capital city is Jerusalem. Over 750,000 people live in Jerusalem. It is a holy city for Jews, Muslims, and Christians.

Many cultural traditions celebrated in Israel are religious. Others remember an important day in history or carry on a long-standing custom. This book looks at the cultural traditions of Israel from January to December. However, in Israel, holidays follow the lunar calendar. The lunar calendar follows the stages of the Moon. This means that holidays do not always happen at the same time each year.

Did You Know?
When a Jewish boy turns 13, his birthday is celebrated with a special party called a bar mitzvah. When a girl turns 12, she has a bat mitzvah. These celebrations represent the beginning of adulthood for boys and girls.

New Year for Trees

In January or early February, Tu Bishvat, also known as New Year for Trees, is celebrated in Israel. Trees have an important meaning for the Jewish people. They are a symbol for life. During this festival, people across the country plant trees and remember the importance of nature.

Tu Bishvat is similar to Arbor Day in other parts of the world.

On Tu Bishvat, it is traditional to eat different kinds of fruit grown in Israel. After eating any fruit, many people say blessings. In the **Torah**, seven kinds of fruit are given special importance. They are known as the *Shivat Haminim*, or Seven Species. The seven species are wheat, barley, grapes, figs, pomegranates, olives, and dates.

These are some of the traditional fruits eaten on Tu Bishvat.

Did You Know?
In Hebrew, *Tu* means 15, and Shevat is a month on the Jewish calendar.

Purim

Purim is one of the happiest holidays in Israel. It usually takes place in March. During this springtime celebration, people remember the story of Queen Esther saving the Jewish people from an evil **tyrant** named Haman. Haman was plotting to kill all the Jewish people. Purim celebrates a time when Jewish people were saved from being completely destroyed.

Did You Know?
The largest Purim parade in Israel takes place in a city called Holon. There are dancers, acrobats, jugglers, and huge colorful floats in the parade.

People rejoice and feast during Purim. People eat sweet cakes filled with prunes or poppy seeds. Adults drink wine, and children dress up in costumes or wear masks. Some people make gift baskets for their friends and neighbors. Others give money to the poor.

The streets are filled with children in costumes during Purim. Many girls dress up as Queen Esther.

Hamantaschen, a Purim treat, are triangle-shaped pastries.

9

Passover

During Passover, Israelis celebrate the Exodus, which is the story of how Jewish slaves in Egypt escaped to freedom. Families gather to remember their **ancestors**' escape from slavery and to celebrate their freedom.

Did You Know?
Passover lasts for seven days in Israel. Jewish people in other parts of the world celebrate for eight days.

Long ago, the Jews who escaped from slavery baked thin, flat bread called *matzah* or *matzo* in the hot desert sun. They did not have time to let their bread rise as they fled from Egypt. People still eat flat bread during Passover. People also enjoy a meal called a Seder. During the Seder, a special plate is prepared with foods to remind people of the hardships of the Jews when they were slaves.

Matzah looks and tastes like a cracker.

Many Jewish families have special dishes, glasses, and silverware that are only used for Seder.

Memorial Days

Near the end of April or the beginning of May, Israel's Day of Remembrance of the **Holocaust** and Heroism is held. On this day, Israelis remember the six million Jews killed by the Nazis during World War II. They also remember and honor the many Jews who acted bravely during this sad time in history.

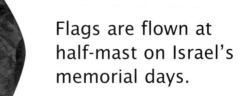

Flags are flown at half-mast on Israel's memorial days.

Statues and other tributes are displayed at the Holocaust Memorial in Israel.

Israel's National Memorial Day also takes place in spring, one week after Holocaust Remembrance Day. This is a day to remember all of Israel's soldiers and other people who have died for their country.

Did You Know?
Memorial services are held throughout Israel for Holocaust Remembrance Day and Israel's Memorial Day. Special sirens are sounded, and everyone must stop what they are doing and stand in silence. Cars and other vehicles stop at the side of the road.

Independence Day

Israelis celebrate Independence Day one day after Memorial Day. This is the national day of Israel, celebrating the Israeli Declaration of Independence in 1948. Some people go to a special ceremony in Jerusalem. Others gather with their families and have picnics on hillsides and other beautiful spots throughout the country. They build bonfires and join together to sing and to tell stories.

Families gather from all over Israel, and even other countries, for Independence Day parties.

Most businesses are closed on Independence Day, but cafés, restaurants, movie theaters, and other places of entertainment are open because it is not a religious holiday.

Many cities throughout Israel hold outdoor performances featuring fireworks displays and famous Israeli singers.

Did You Know?
On Independence Day, people decorate their balconies and car windows with Israeli flags. The Star of David, an important Jewish symbol, appears on the Israeli flag.

Shavuot

During Shavuot, Israelis celebrate the anniversary of the day long ago when God gave the Jewish people the Torah at Mount Sinai. The holiday is known as the festival of the giving of the Torah. People study and read from the Torah during Shavuot.

Torah scrolls are usually kept in special containers to protect them.

Shavuot also celebrates the harvest of grains, including wheat and barley. People also give thanks for other foods, such as grapes, figs, pomegranates, olives, and dates. It is a tradition to eat milk and cheese on Shavuot. People also decorate their homes and **synagogues** with fruits and flowers to celebrate the harvest.

Did You Know?
Shavuot, Passover, and Sukkot are three **pilgrimage** festivals. In ancient times, Jewish people would gather in Jerusalem for these special festivals and bring offerings to the **temple.**

Shavuot celebrations last one day.

Ramadan

Many Muslims in Israel celebrate the month-long holiday of Ramadan. Muslims believe in the religion of Islam. During Ramadan, they celebrate their faith, their families, and their communities. They also celebrate and read from the Quran, which is the Muslim holy book.

Muslims are allowed to work during Ramadan, but they do not eat, drink, or even chew gum during daylight hours.

Children do not have to fast during Ramadan, but many try to fast for some of the time.

During Ramadan, adults and teenagers **fast**. They do not eat or drink anything from sunrise to sunset. Special prayer services are held at **mosques**. They fast to purify their minds and bodies. They also fast to remind themselves of what it feels like to have no food or water.

Day of Mourning

In July or August, Israelis have a day off work and school to remember and **mourn** the destruction of their first and second temples long ago. They also mourn the **exile** of the Jews from Israel long ago. This sad day is called Tisha B'Av.

On Tisha B'Av, many Jewish people visit cemeteries to mourn family members who have died.

During Tisha B'Av, many people restrict their activities to commemorate past tragedies of the Jewish people. Some fast and visit cemeteries. People do not listen to music or take showers or baths on this day. Some Jews read from the **Book of Lamentations** by candlelight, while sitting on the floor. Some Jews even sleep on the floor on Tisha B'Av.

Did You Know?
On Tisha B'Av, many Israelis go to the Western Wall in Jerusalem, the only wall left of the Second Temple. They read Lamentations to show their sadness.

21

Rosh Hashanah

Rosh Hashanah is the celebration of the Jewish New Year. This two-day festival usually takes place in September or October. During Rosh Hashanah, Jews reflect on their actions and behavior in the past year. They also think about how they can improve themselves in the year to come. People wish one another a happy new year in Hebrew by saying "Shana Tova!"

Did You Know?
During Rosh Hashanah, people eat a round loaf of bread called *challah*. They dip pieces of bread in honey so they will have a sweet year.

Some prayers are held at the beach on Rosh Hashanah. People have the day off work and school.

Jews also remember the creation of the world during Rosh Hashanah. They believe that God made the world during this time. On the evening of the beginning of Rosh Hashanah, many Jews eat sweet foods including sliced apples and honey. Many go to synagogues to pray for a sweet and happy year ahead.

Yom Kippur

For many Israelis, Yom Kippur is the most important and holiest day of the entire year. People pray to be forgiven for any wrongdoings and feel closest to God. Yom Kippur takes place ten days after Rosh Hashanah. The days in between these holidays are called the Days of Awe.

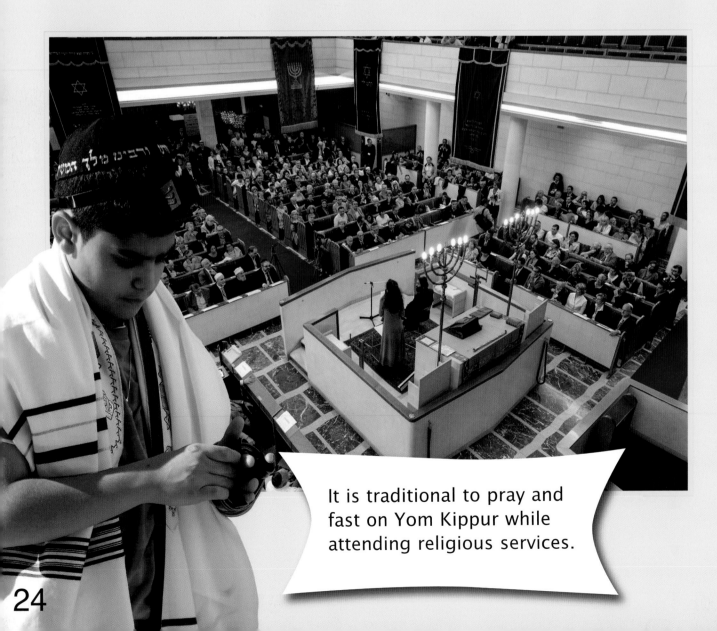

It is traditional to pray and fast on Yom Kippur while attending religious services.

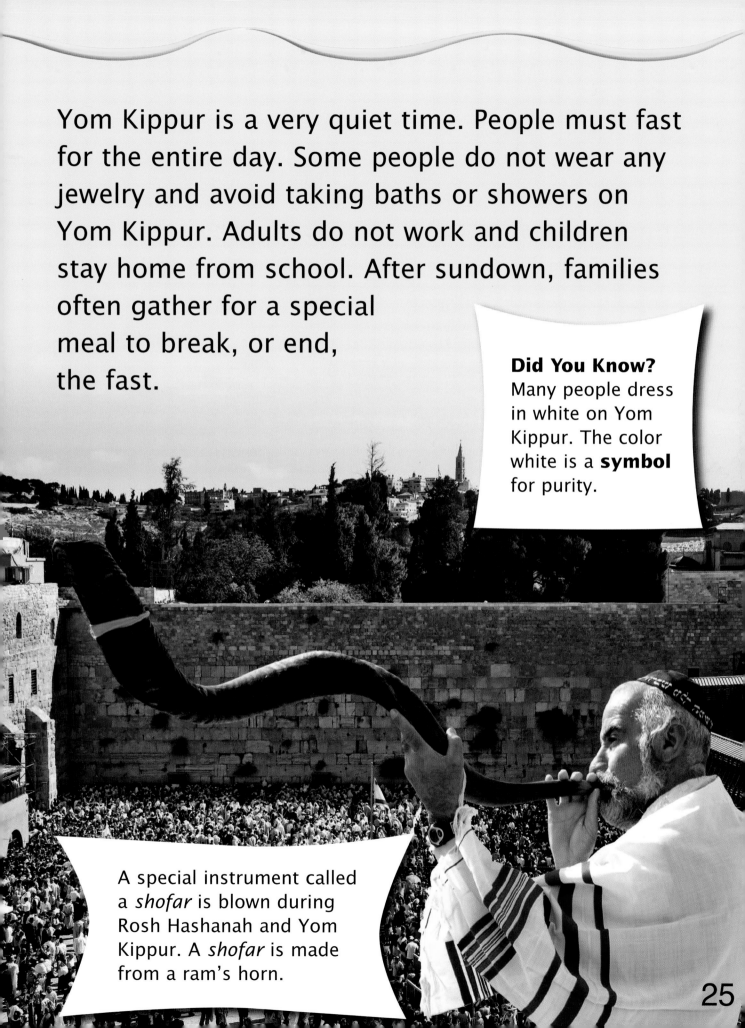

Yom Kippur is a very quiet time. People must fast for the entire day. Some people do not wear any jewelry and avoid taking baths or showers on Yom Kippur. Adults do not work and children stay home from school. After sundown, families often gather for a special meal to break, or end, the fast.

Did You Know?
Many people dress in white on Yom Kippur. The color white is a **symbol** for purity.

A special instrument called a *shofar* is blown during Rosh Hashanah and Yom Kippur. A *shofar* is made from a ram's horn.

25

Sukkot

People all over Israel celebrate the harvest season during the holiday of Sukkot. This week-long holiday usually takes place in September or October. During Sukkot, people build sukkot, or huts made of branches and leaves, in the yards of synagogues and of their homes. For the seven days of Sukkot, families eat dinner and say blessings in their **sukkah**. Some people even sleep in the sukkah.

Families often use palm branches to cover the open-air roof of a sukkah. Then they hang up decorations.

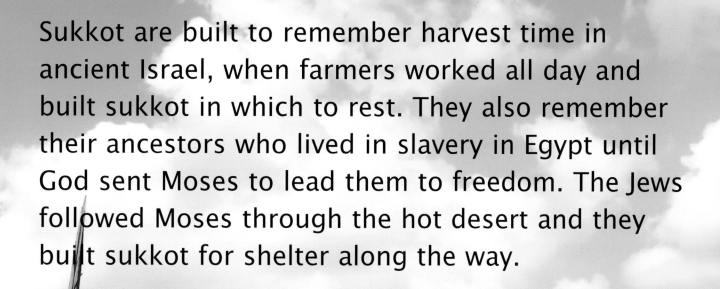

Sukkot are built to remember harvest time in ancient Israel, when farmers worked all day and built sukkot in which to rest. They also remember their ancestors who lived in slavery in Egypt until God sent Moses to lead them to freedom. The Jews followed Moses through the hot desert and they built sukkot for shelter along the way.

Did You Know?
Israelis celebrate a good harvest of avocados, figs, apricots, citrus fruits, and peppers during Sukkot.

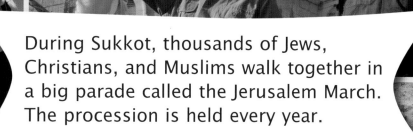

During Sukkot, thousands of Jews, Christians, and Muslims walk together in a big parade called the Jerusalem March. The procession is held every year.

Simchat Torah

Sukkot ends with a festival called Simchat Torah. The Torah is the holy book of Judaism. It is known as the Jewish Bible and is read from beginning to end every year. Simchat Torah celebrates the completion of the yearly reading of the Torah.

The Torah is written on parchment, a paper-like material that is rolled into a scroll.

Did You Know?
Jewish holidays begin at sundown and end when the sun sets the next day.

During Simchat Torah, the very last section of the Torah is read. It is a time for great celebration. In synagogues, there is singing and dancing and the Torah is carried around. As soon as the last section is finished, the reading of the Torah starts again from the beginning.

Hanukkah

Hanukkah takes place in winter in November or December. It is also known as the Festival of Lights. People light candles and remember an important event in Jewish history. Over 2,000 years ago, an evil king would not let Jewish people practice their religion. He took over their temple in Jerusalem. A small group of Jewish soldiers fought back against the king's army. Their leader was named Judah Maccabee and his soldiers were called the Maccabees. After many battles, the Maccabees took back their temple and the Jewish people were free to practice their religion once again.

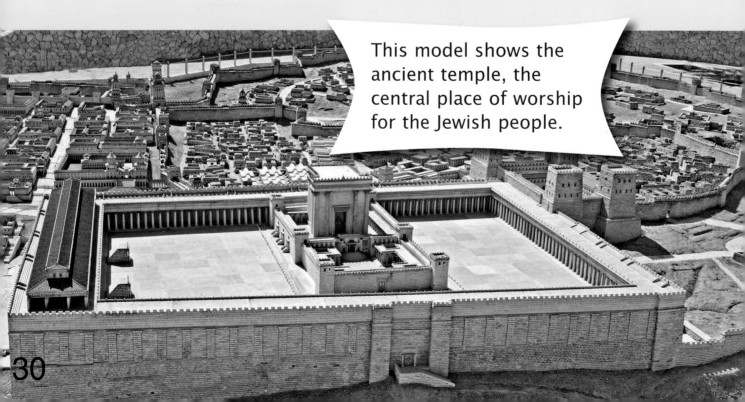

This model shows the ancient temple, the central place of worship for the Jewish people.

Did You Know?
Hanukkah lasts for eight days.
People light one candle for each day
in a candle-holder called a menorah.

Today, family members
celebrate Hanukkah
together. They gather
together for special
meals and children
receive gifts from
their parents.

Glossary

ancestors People from whom others are descended

Book of Lamentations An Old Testament section that expresses sorrow for the destruction of Jerusalem

exile Being forced to leave one's country or home

fast To go without eating or drinking

Holocaust The widespread killing of Jewish people during World War II

mosques Places where Muslims worship

mourn To feel or show grief or sadness

pilgrimage A journey

sukkah A temporary hut made of branches built for Sukkot

symbol Something that stands for or represents something else

synagogues Places where Jewish people worship

temple A special building for worship

Torah The holy book of Judaism

tyrant A harsh or cruel ruler

Index